This
alphabet
in disguise

has words
to the
wise

color
for the
eyes

and
pictures
of surprise.

I'll teach you the rules,
so you can break the rules,
and then teach me new rules.

ISBN 0-9656782-1-0

Copyright © 1999 JAY PALEFSKY   All rights reserved.

Kutzkies Artworks
1050 Old Albany Post Rd.
Garrison, NY 10524

email: kutzkies@highlands.com
web: www.kutzkies.com

These 10,000 copies were made in the U.S.A.
Printed by Merchants Press on recycled paper.

JOSHUA & SARAH, MOM AND I LOVE GROWING UP LAUGHING WITH BOTH OF YOU.

WRITTEN AND ILLUSTRATED BY JAY PALEFSKY

Arnie Dillo always stayed home
And Buffy Lo wanted to roam.
She was content while he liked to gripe
so they became the marrying type.

Bo Constrictor

Bo and Aro were aiming high for a wedding in mid-July, when their love would be so ripe for them to become man(eater) and vipe.

Buffy Lo

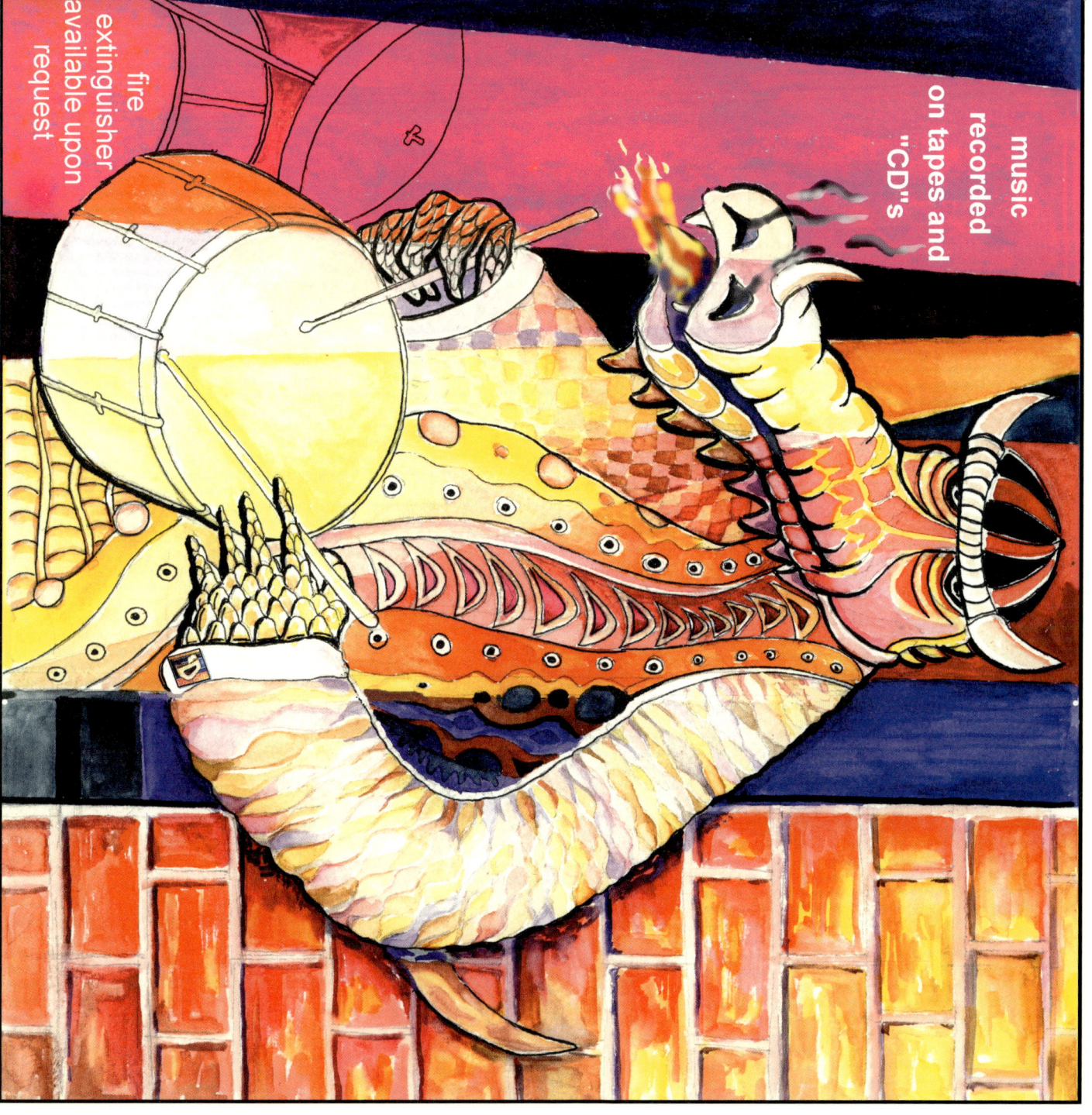

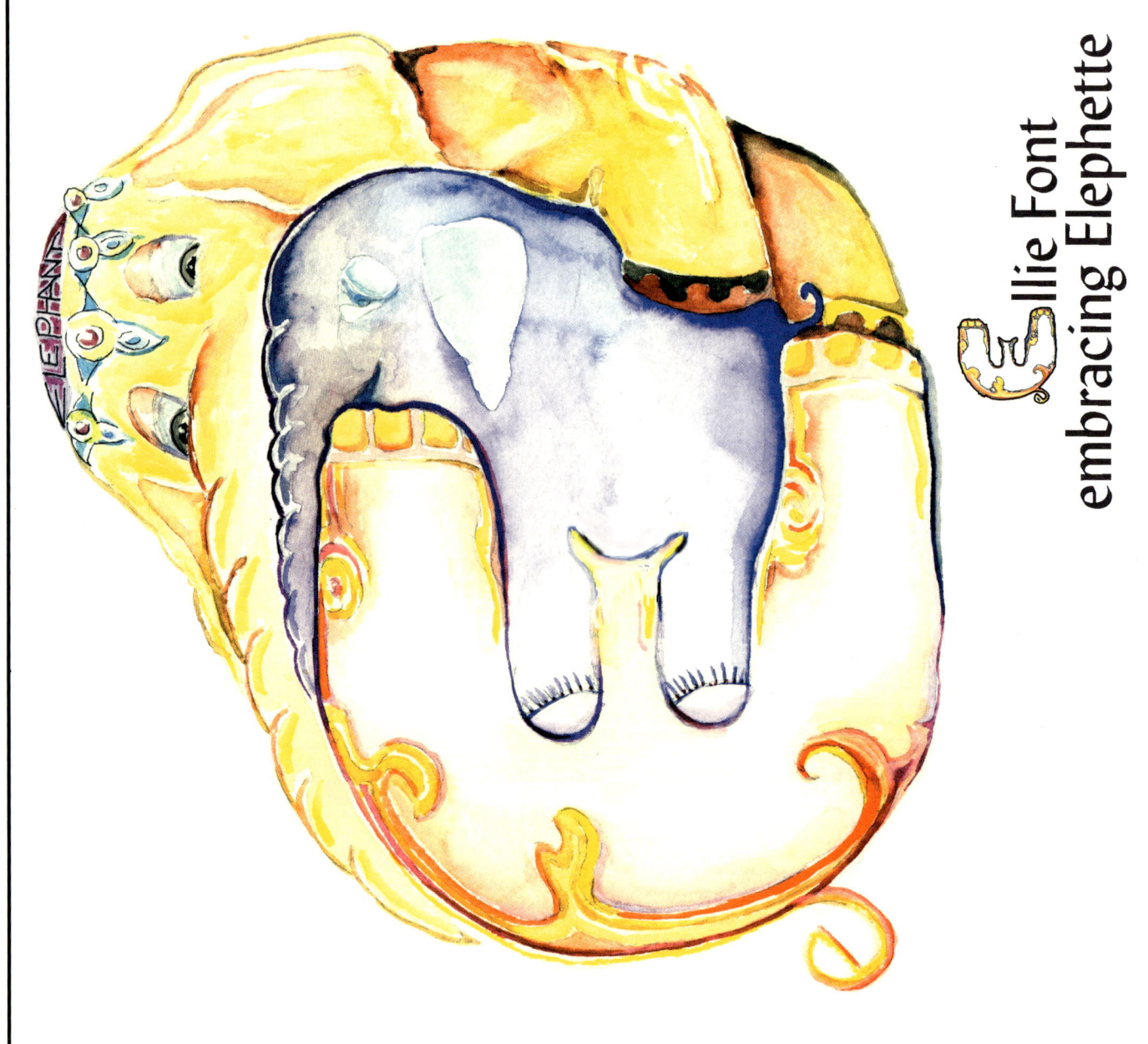

Ellie Font embracing Elephette

Elves and Fairies and
morning-glories and
children and dreams and
make-believe stories and
colors and wonders and
magical sights and
elephants and frogs and
funtastic delights.

Glowing Hearts
Golden Fishes
Hobby Horses
Hopeful Wishes
Galloping Higher
Heading Out To See
Galleries Of Adventure
Horizons Set Free

ester juggling jewels

King Knowing was looking for his Lady "L" knowing all too well that she could get lost in his lonesome kingdom.

ady "L" let the king find her by lighting up the lonely landscape. They lived forever after "Knowing Love".

arty Parade

queen quail

Rabbit royale

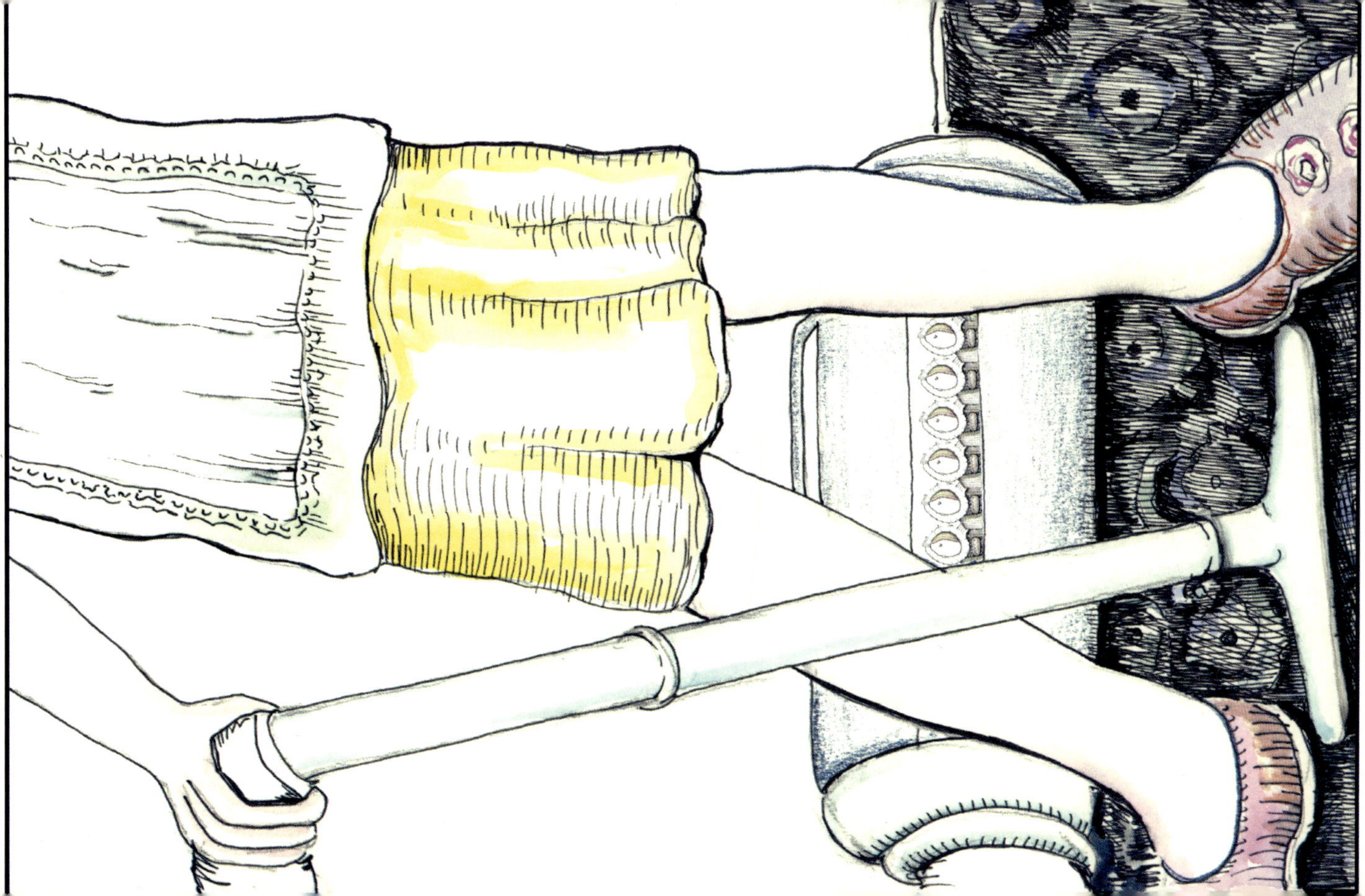

"I won't RQ with you. I will quit reading and QUEEN up my room."

Shoes
socks
sneakers
shoes
socks
sneakers
shoes
socks
sneakers
shoes
socks
sneakers
shoes
socks
sneakers
SOCKS
SNEAKERS

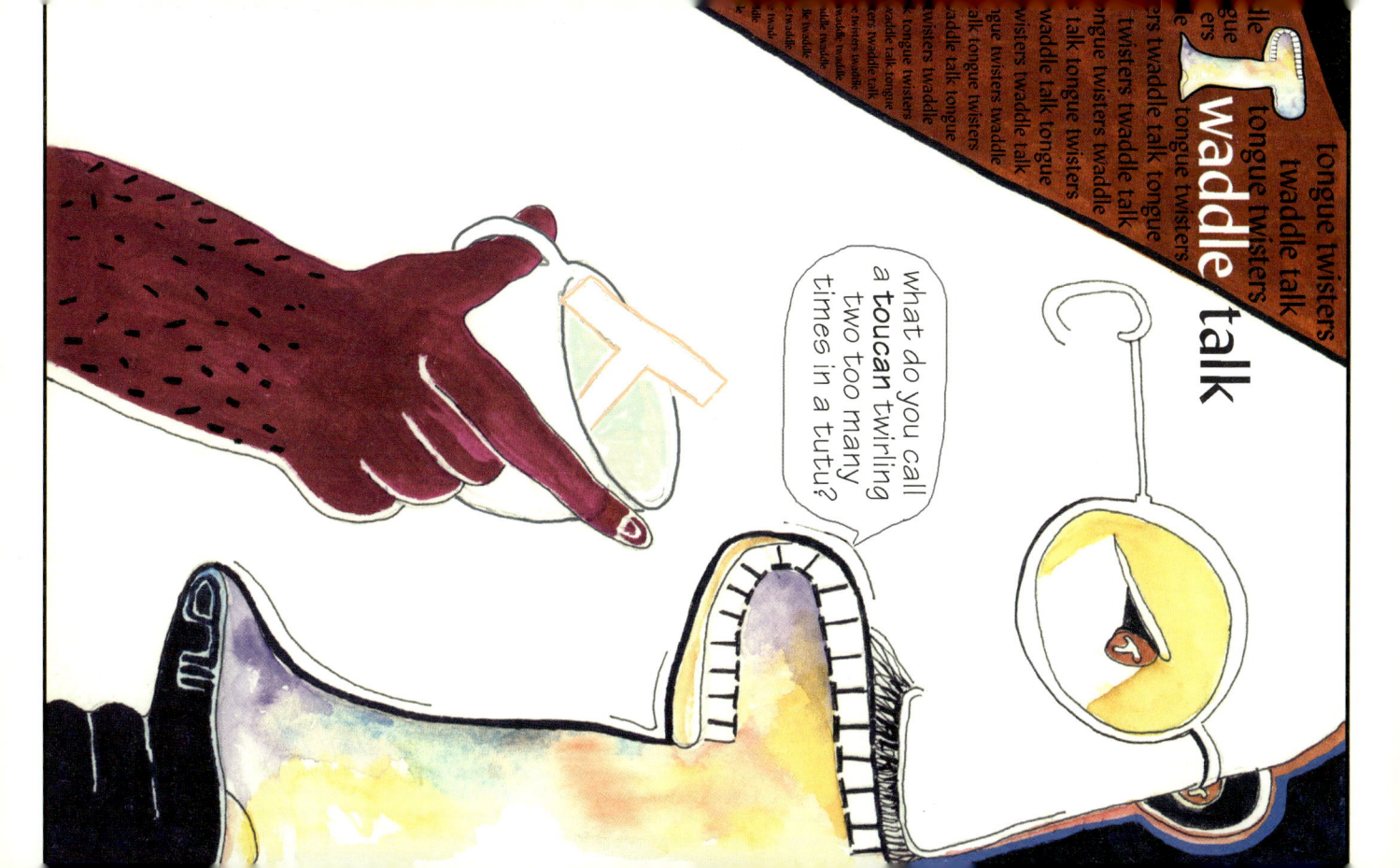

tongue twisters twaddle talk tongue twisters twaddle talk tongue twisters twaddle talk tongue twisters twaddle talk tongue twisters twaddle talk tongue twisters twaddle talk tongue twisters

waddle talk

what do you call a **toucan** twirling two too many times in a tutu?

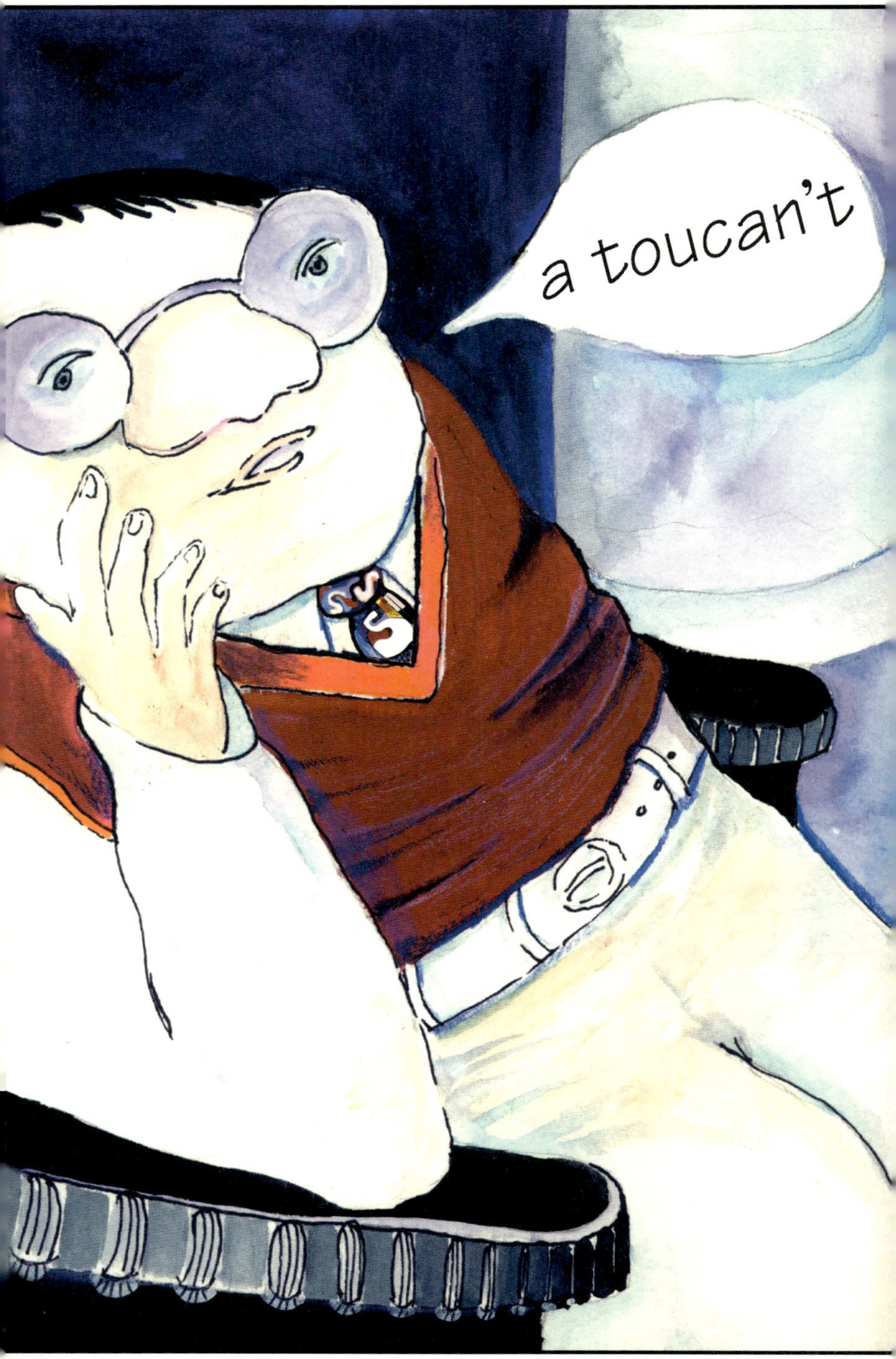
a toucan't

The Shoe Critic

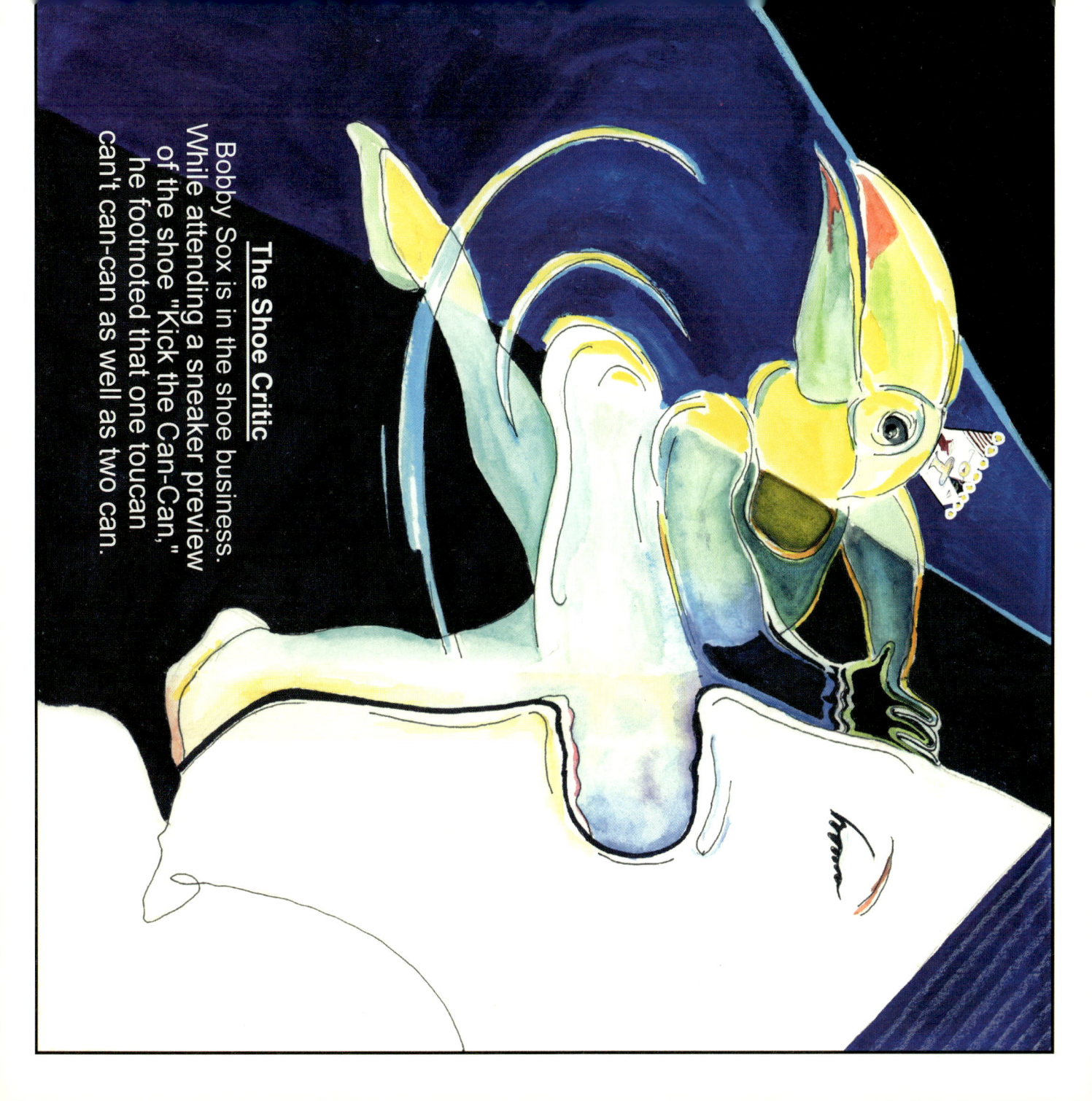

Bobby Sox is in the shoe business. While attending a sneaker preview of the shoe "Kick the Can-Can," he footnoted that one toucan can't can-can as well as two can.

Unique Unicorns

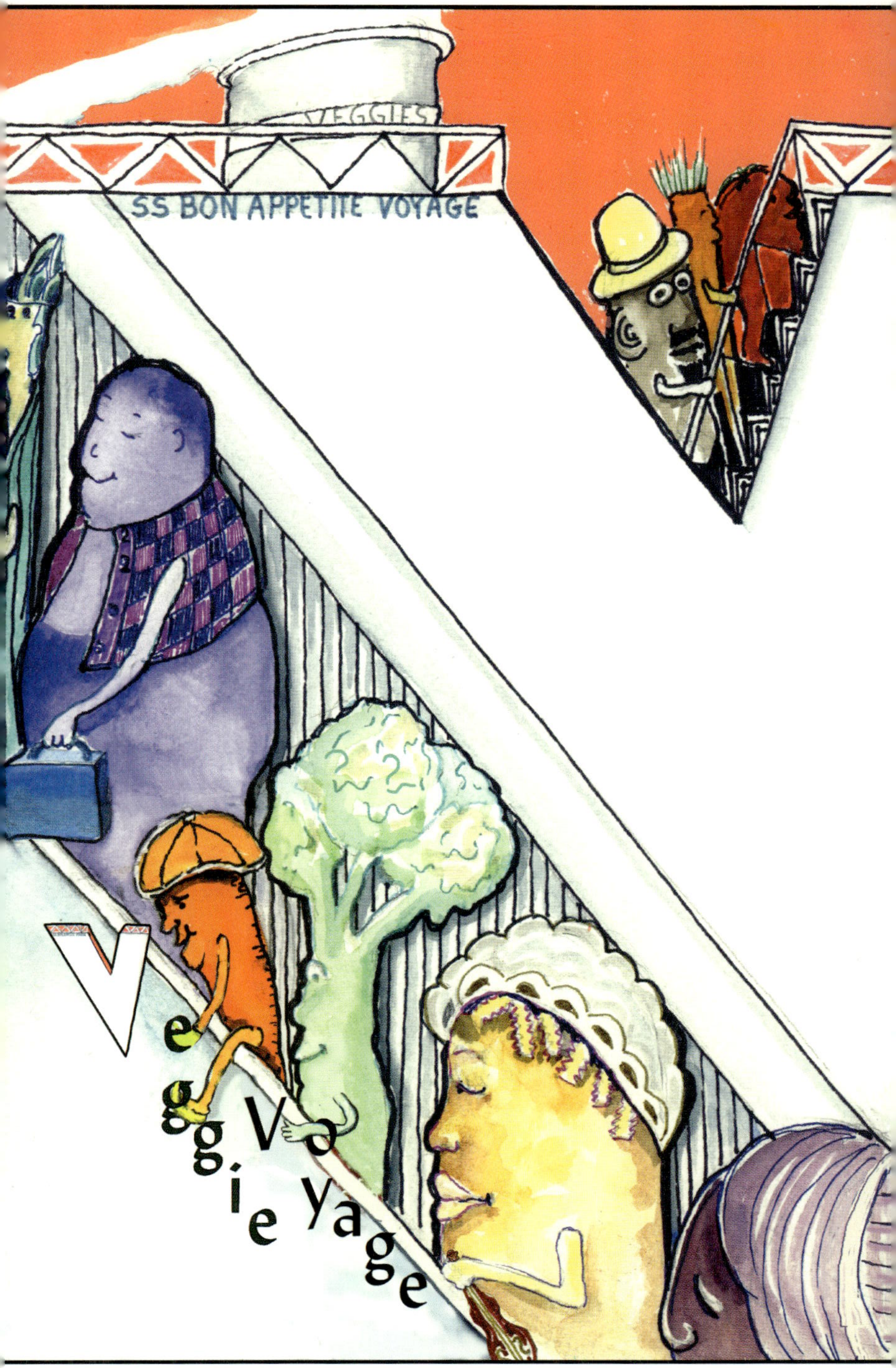
VEGGIES
SS BON APPETITE VOYAGE
Veggie Voyage

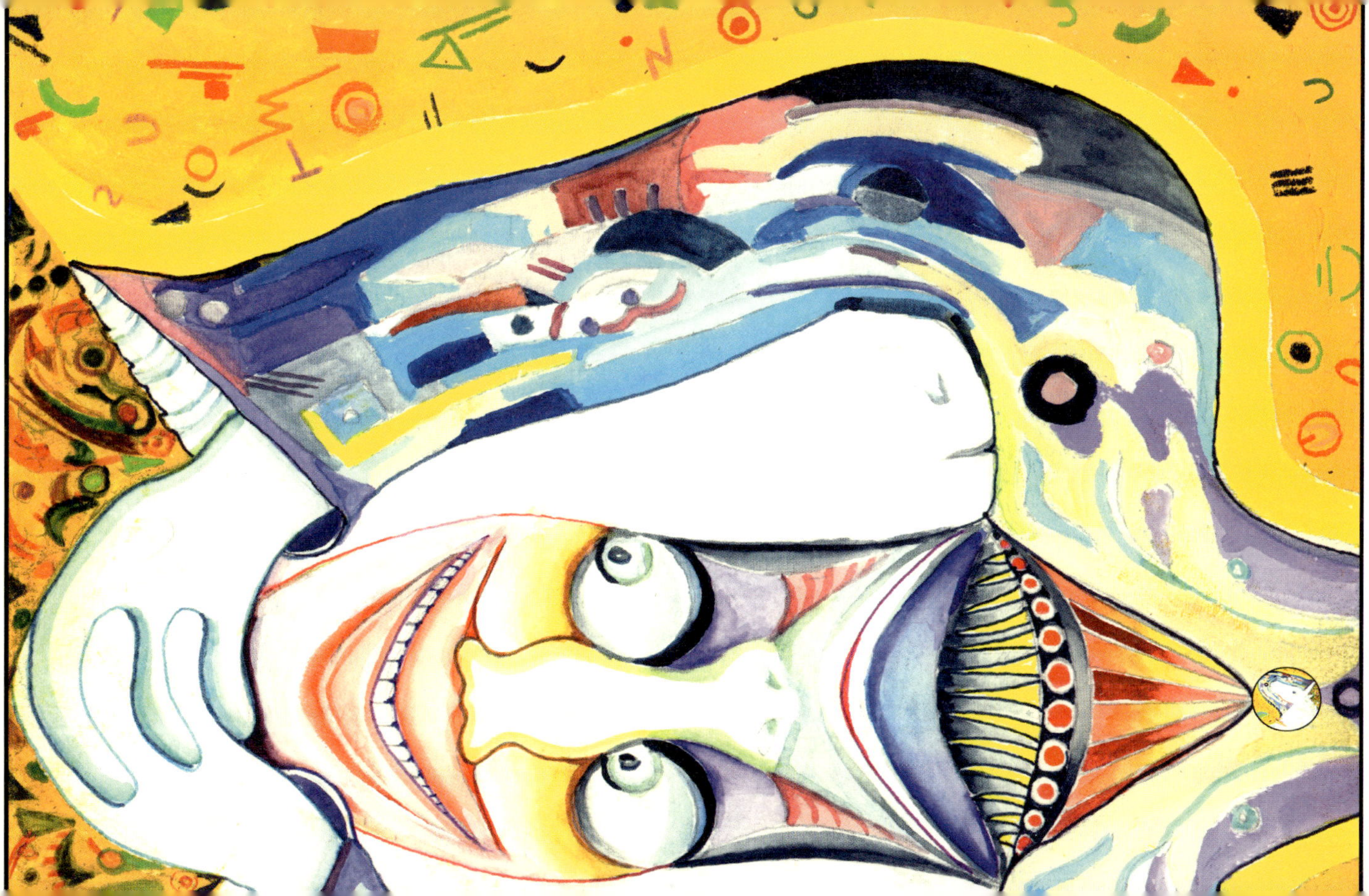

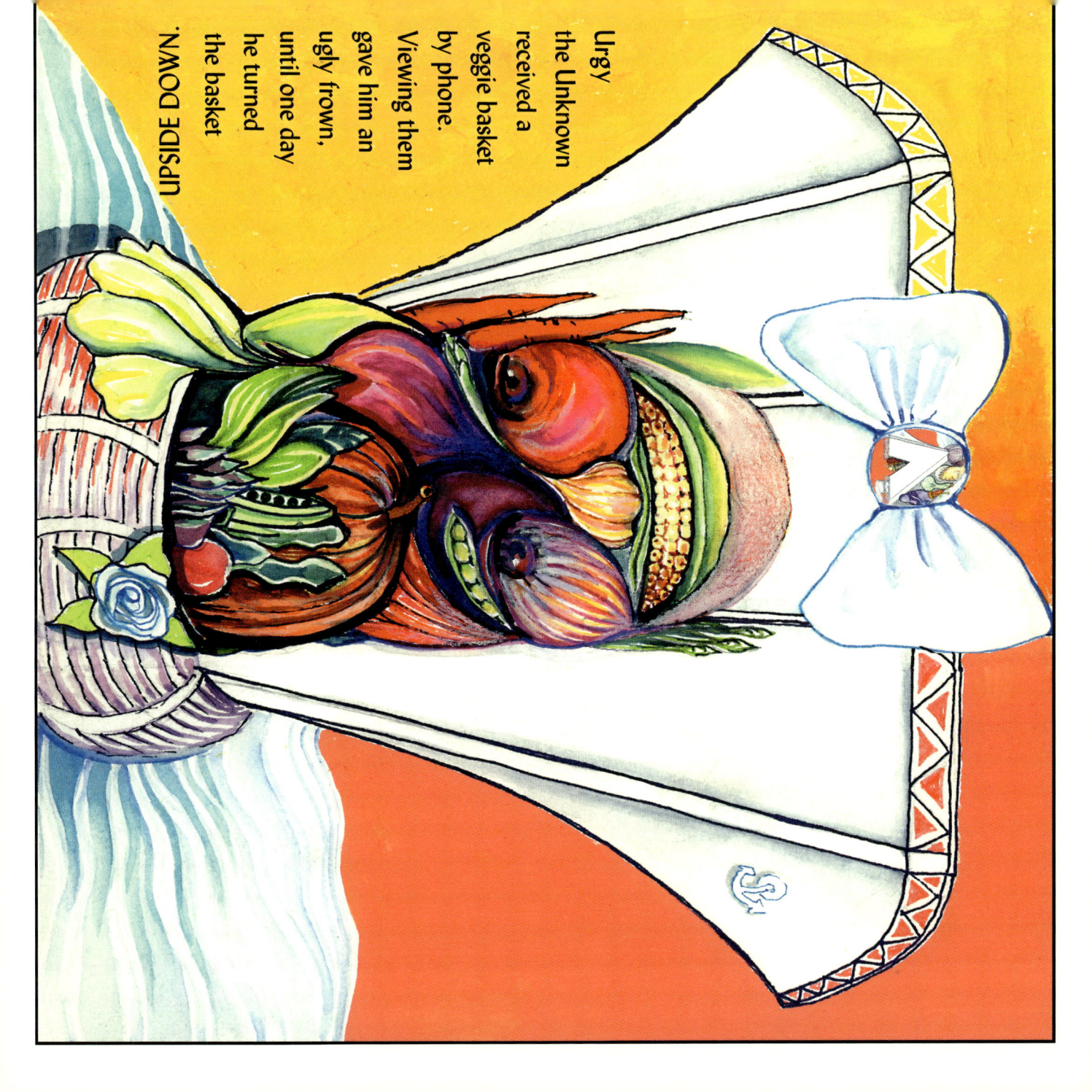

Urgy the Unknown received a veggie basket by phone. Viewing them gave him an ugly frown, until one day he turned the basket UPSIDE DOWN.

Hex the Wizard with his wittle wishy-washy wish watch which was witch-crafted and water*poof* wanted Xyla the Hex to disappear...

Xyla the Hex who was Wex's ex asked a sphinx, a jinx, and a lynx-that-stinx to fix a mix of stix and trix to expel the spell. However...

EXPWOSION

EXTRA EXTRA EXTRA

Wex the Wizard along with his neighbor, Xyla the Hex, both vanished when they tried to outspell each other. Wex left behind his double ewes and Xyla her phone.

XYLA THE HEX

Yellow Y
is on the road

Why is the Y
yellow on the
yellow road?
I yell hi.
I yell low.
I know why.
Do you know
"Y"?

Zoo

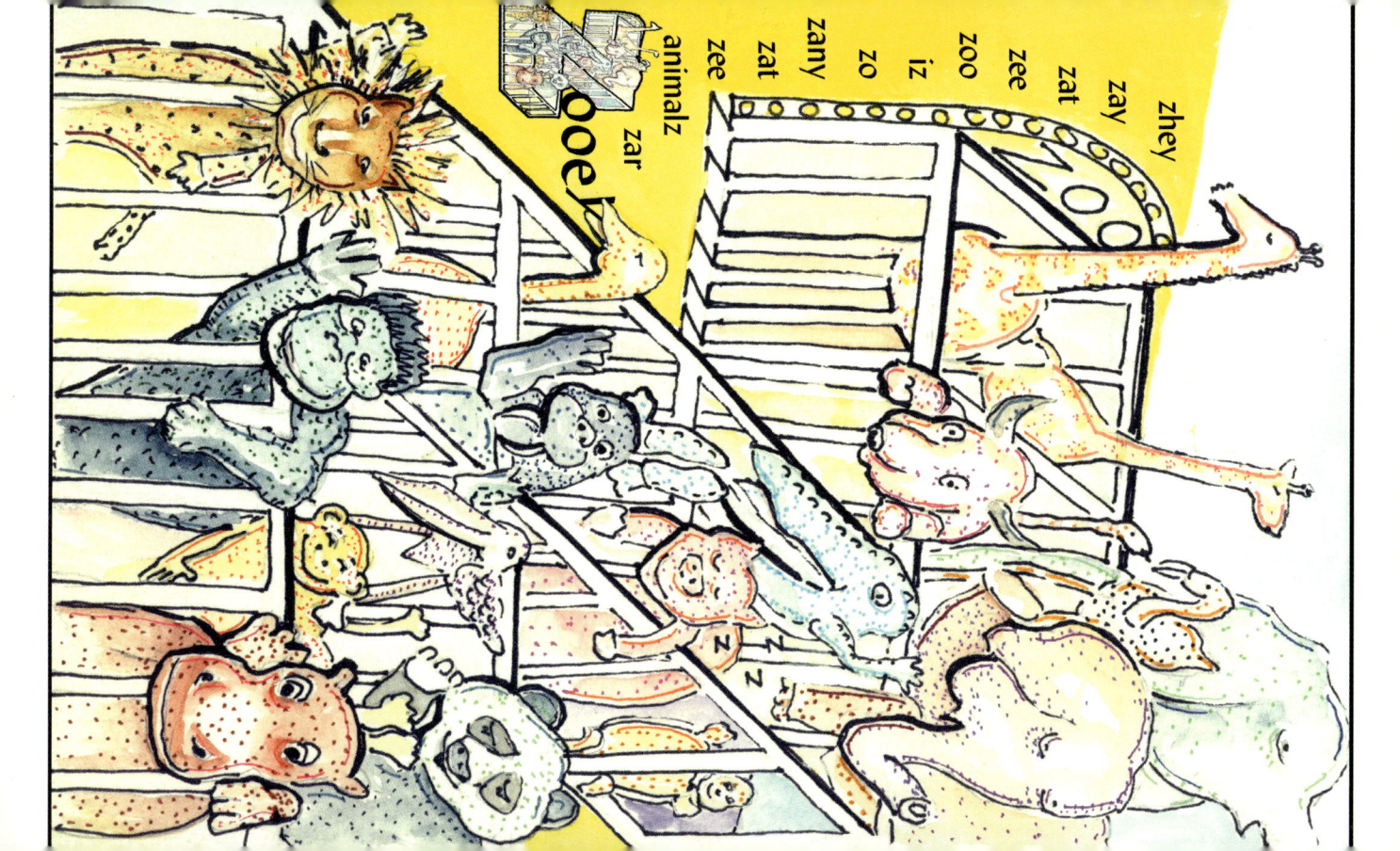

zhey
zay
zat
zee
zoo
iz
zo
zany
zat
zee
animalz
zar

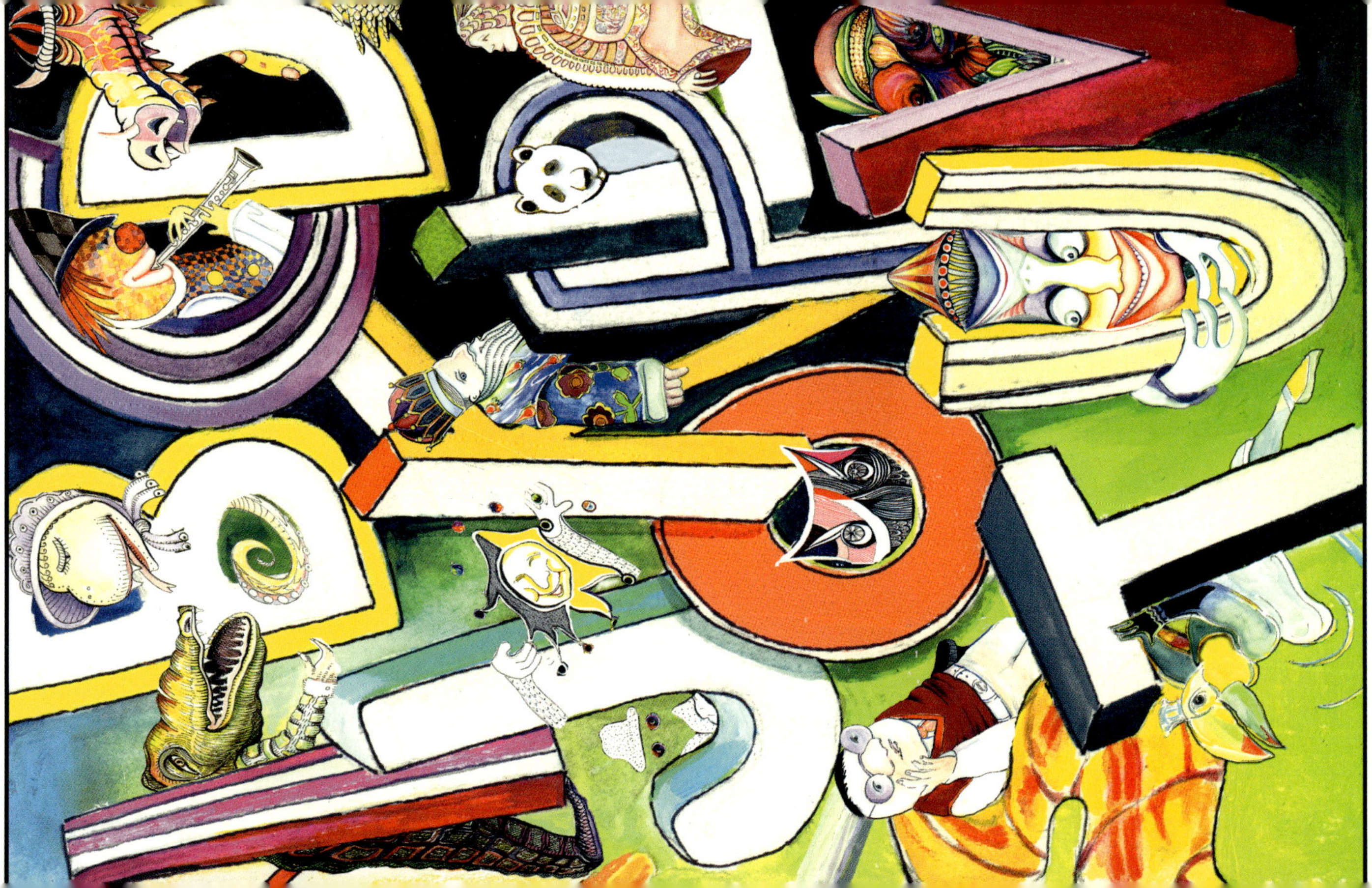

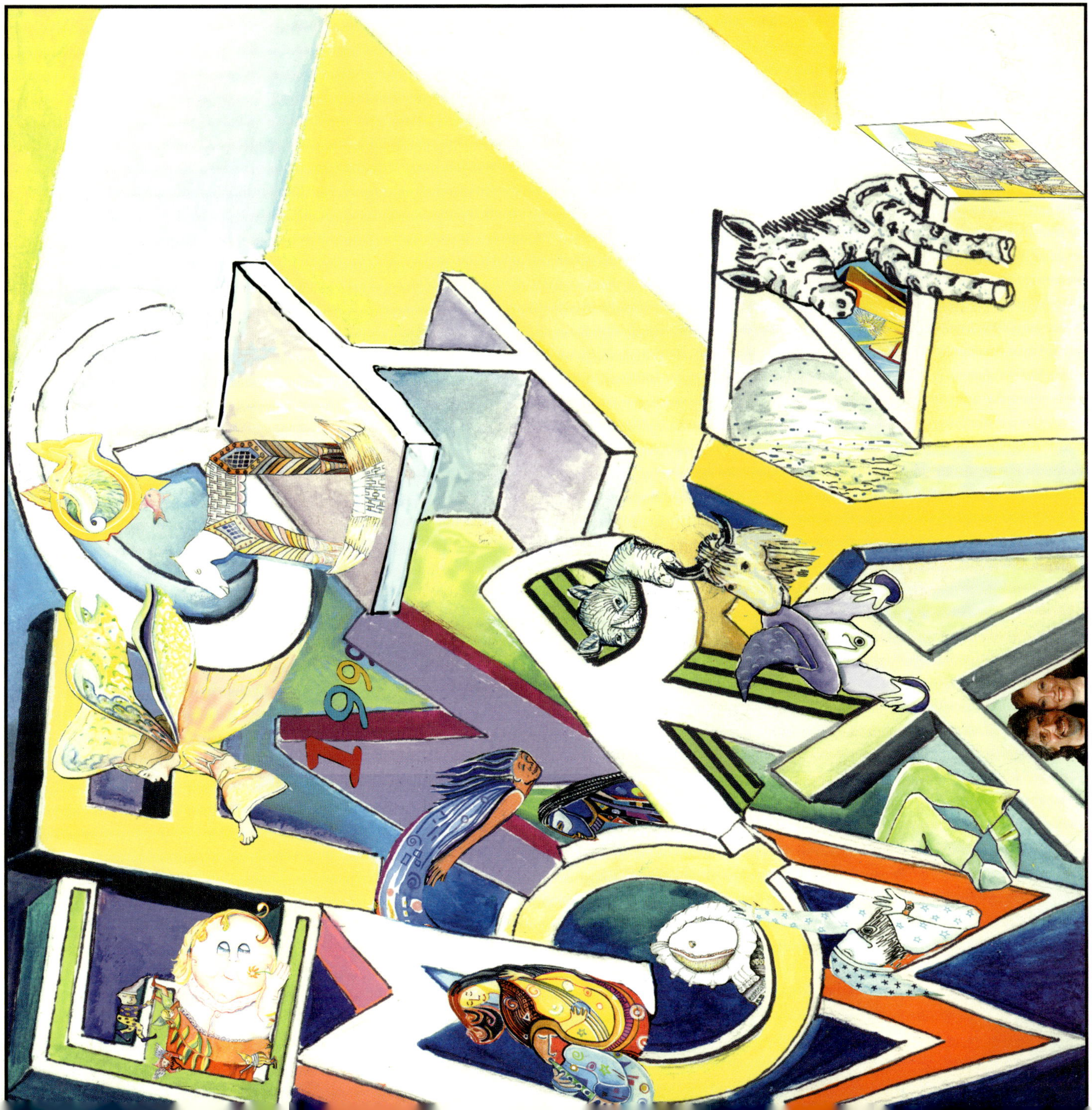
1999

To _____
_____
From _____
Date _____

Acknowledgments:
"Welcome, Baby" by Joan Stimson.
Special thanks to William B. Gurfield, MD.

LADYBIRD BOOKS, INC.
Auburn, Maine 04210 U.S.A.
© LADYBIRD BOOKS LTD 1989
Loughborough, Leicestershire, England

All rights reserved. No part of this publication may be reproduced, stored in a retrieval system, or transmitted in any form or by any means, electronic, mechanical, photocopying, recording or otherwise, without the prior consent of the copyright owner.

Printed in England

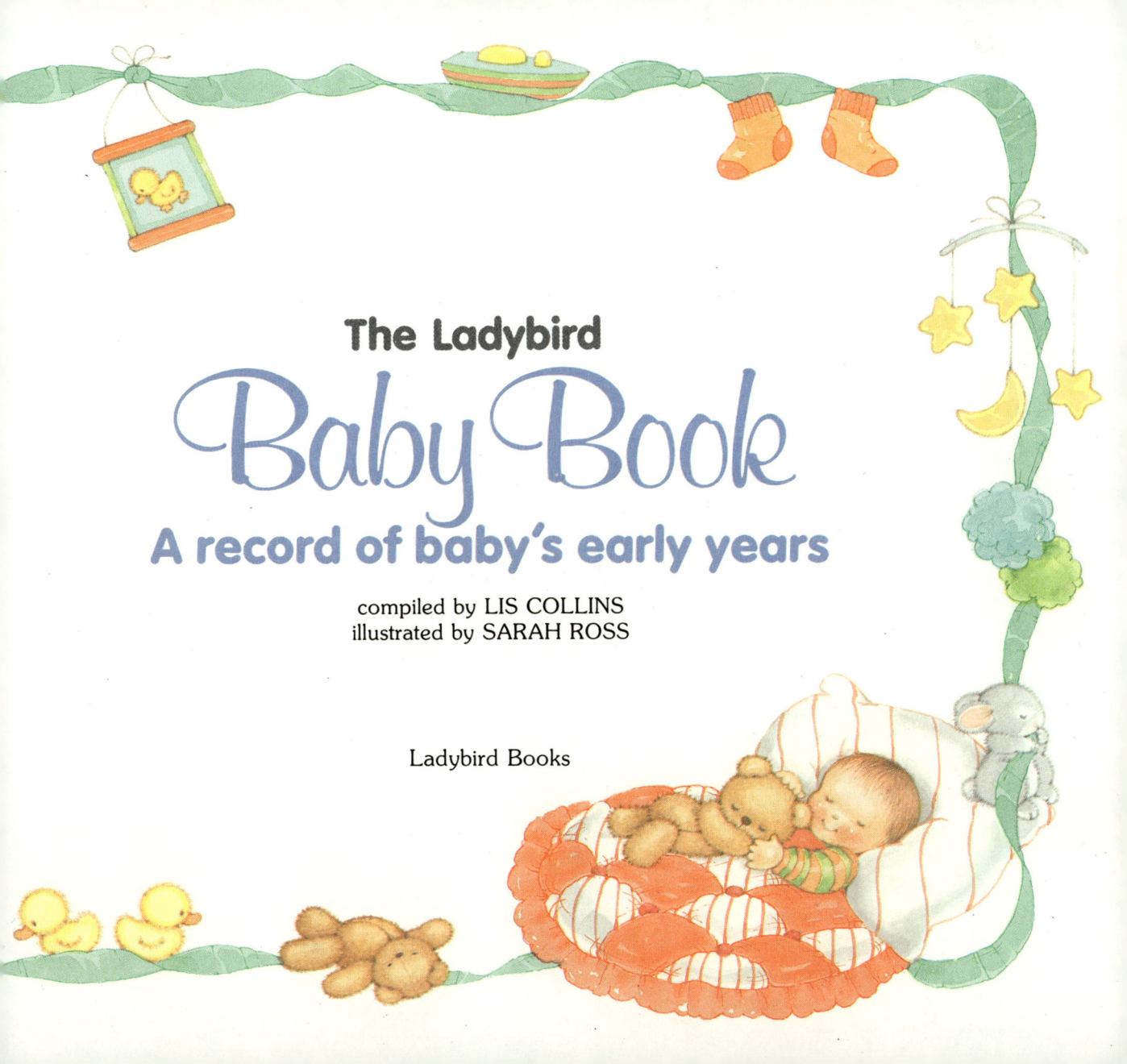

The Ladybird
Baby Book
A record of baby's early years

compiled by LIS COLLINS
illustrated by SARAH ROSS

Ladybird Books

Welcome, baby!
We wish you every joy:
Warm love and light and laughter;
A hug, a kiss, a toy.

Welcome, baby,
To sounds and colors new,
To touch and taste and teddy bears;
They're waiting just for you!

Baby

Name
....

Date due
....

Date of arrival
....

Day of birth
....

Time of birth
....

Birthplace
....

Obstetrician
....

Pediatrician
....

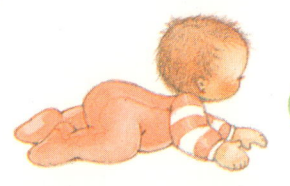

About Me

My Measurements

Age	Height	Weight
......	......	......
......	......	......
......	......	......
......	......	......
......	......	......

Hospital name tag

Lock of hair

Color of eyes

....

Color of hair

....

Resemblances

....

Outline of baby's hand

Outline of baby's foot

When Baby Was Born

Popular songs
....
....

Big names in sports
....
....

Popular TV shows
....
....

Movie of the year
....

News headlines

....

....

Political figures

....

....

Popular fashions

....

....

Milestones

First smiled
....

First slept through the night
....

Cut first tooth
....

Sat up alone
....

Crawled
....

Stood alone
....

Took first steps
....

Spoke first word
....

My Favorite Things

Toys..............................
....
Games............................
....
Stories...........................
....
Songs/rhymes ....
....

Food.............................
....
Animals..........................
....
Friends..........................
....
Special interests ....
....

My Special Words

For family ....
....

For friends ....
....

For animals ....
....

For toys ....
....

For other things
....
....
....
....

My First Mischief

Comments ....
....
....
....
....
....
....
....

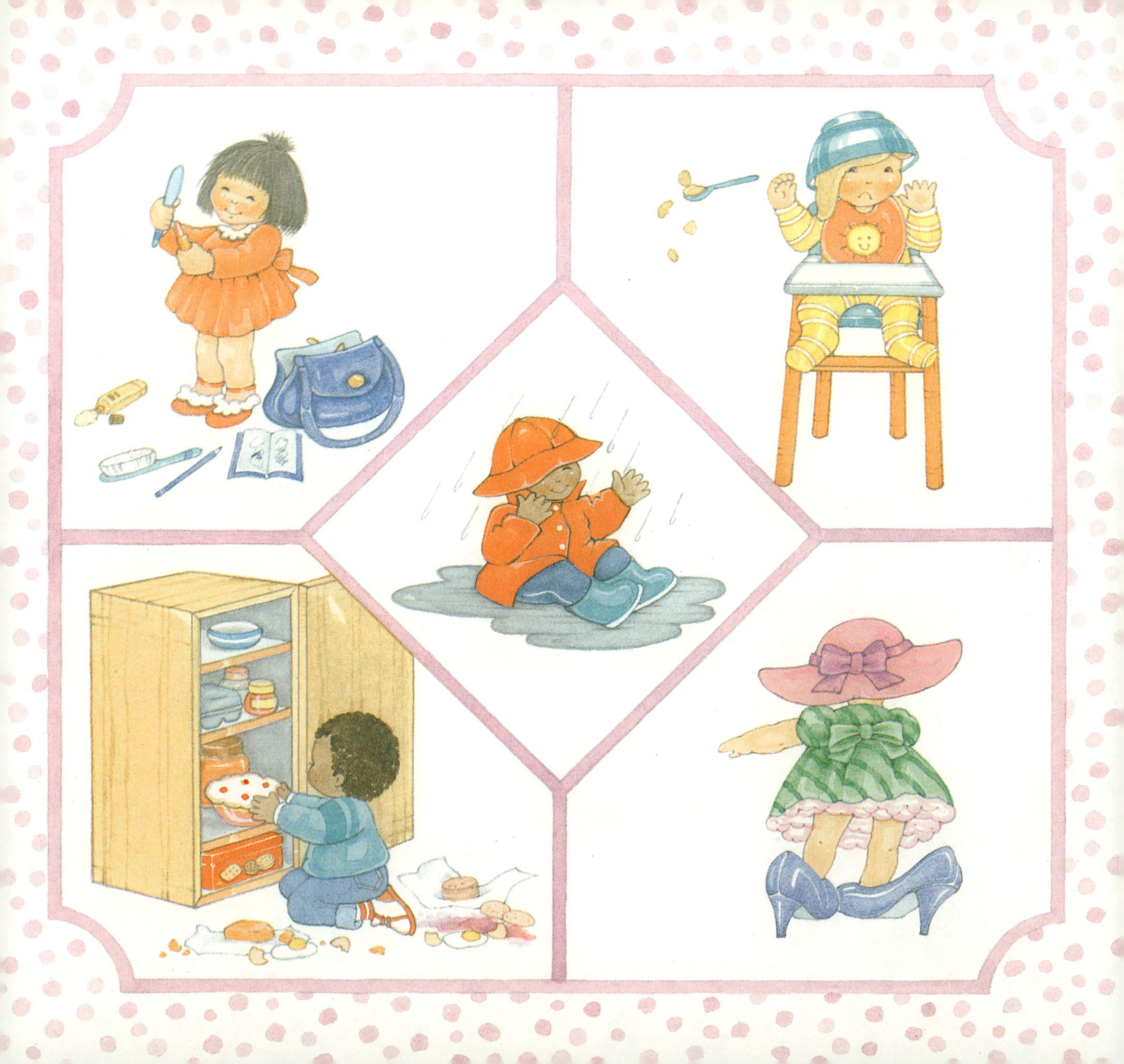

First Christmas

Comments ....
....
....
....
....
....

2nd 3rd

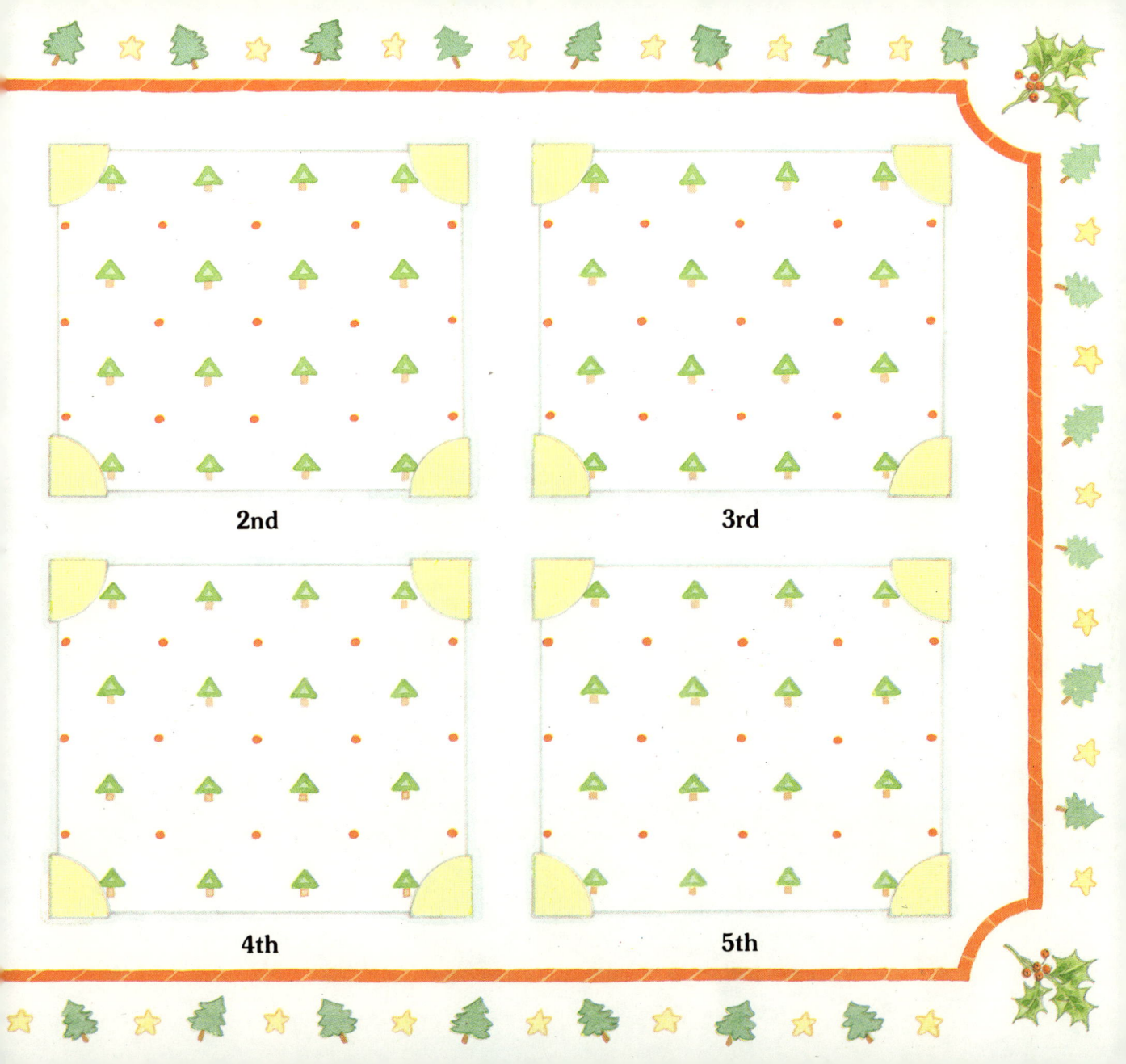

4th 5th

First Birthday

Comments ....
....
....
....
....

2nd

3rd

4th

5th

Vacations and Trips

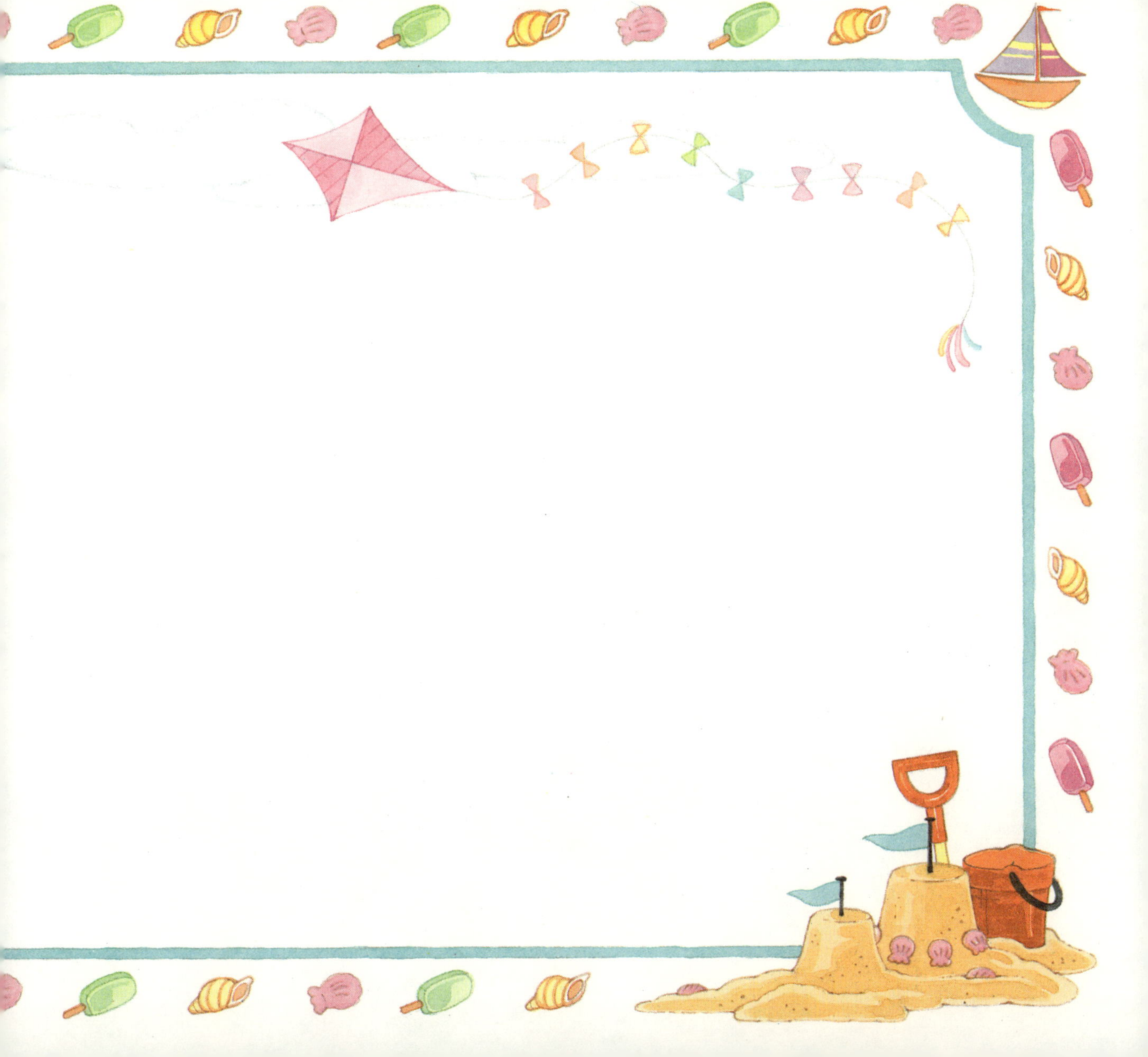

Nursery School

Name of nursery school

....

First day

....

Teacher's name

....

New friends

....

....

....

My First Drawing

Date..

Starting School

Name of school

....

First day

....

Teacher's name

....

New friends ....

....

My Own Writing

....

....

....

....

....

Write your child's name and address for him or her to copy.

Pictures of Me

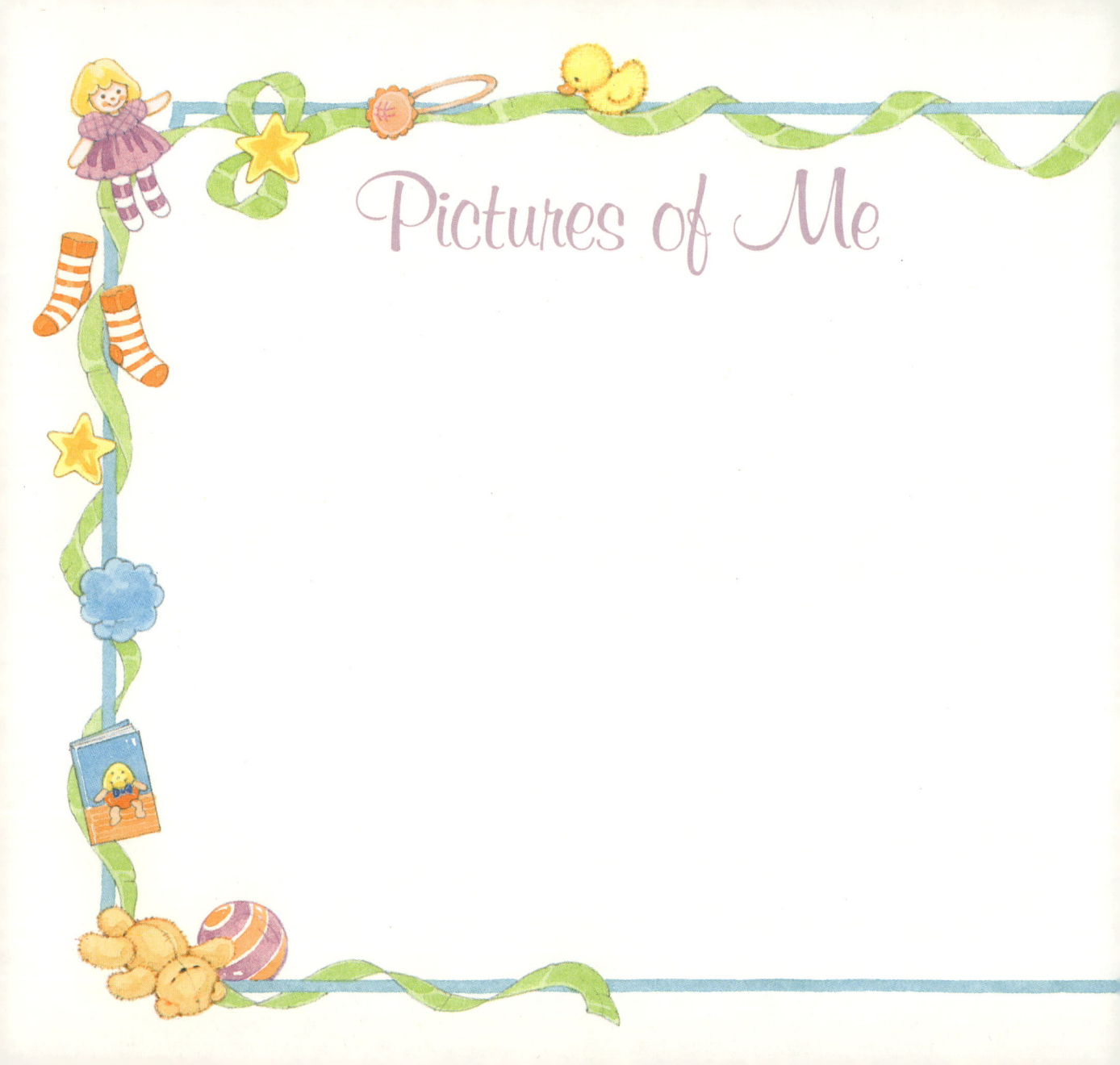

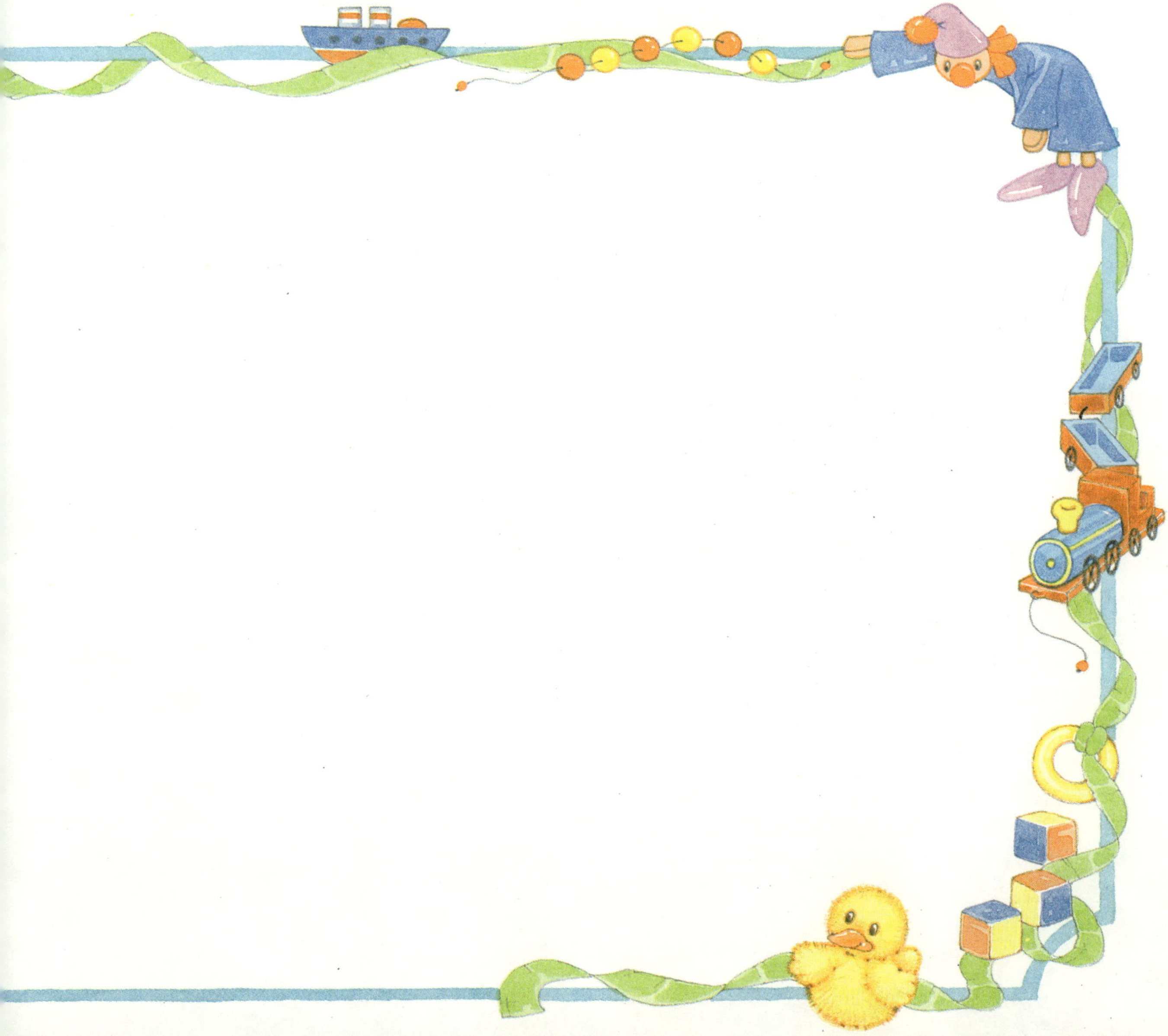

Medical Record

Immunizations	Date	Age
DPT series (Diphtheria, Pertussis, Tetanus)	....	....
Polio	....	....
MMR (Measles, Mumps, Rubella)	....	....
Meningitis (Hemophilus Influenza b)	....	....
Others	....	....
Boosters	....	....